As I am

by
ANNA ADIDEPVORAPHAN

As I am

Copyright © 2020 by Anna Adidepvoraphan.

Paperback ISBN: 978-1-952982-50-7
Ebook ISBN: 978-1-952982-53-8

All rights reserved. No part in this book may be produced and transmitted in any form or by any means, electronic, or mechanical, including photocopying, recording, or by any information storage and retrieval system, without permission in writing from the copyright owner.

The views expressed in this work are solely those of the author and do not necessarily reflect the views of the publisher hereby disclaims any responsibility for them.

Published by Green Sage Agency   11/19/2020

Green Sage Agency
1-888-366-9989
inquiry@greensageagency.com

foreword

"I am okay. There is nothing wrong with me. I don't need to be fixed. But that can't be right. Because ... Because .... Because ...."

Yes, all my past came into play. I held on to them for dear life that I thought they were my truth. Now I see them and recognize them for what they truly are. I see myself clearly.

I can, now accept myself as I am. Nothing more. Nothing less. No why. No how. No maybe.

I simply am. And that is enough.

Anna Adidepvoraphan

Everything that comes alive
Everything that dies inside
It is of my own making
It is of my own choosing

🌀 8th October 2013

I am nothing
I am everything
I am no one
I am everyone

I am the creator
I am the maker
I am the author
Of every minute detail of my life

© 18th February, 2014

I stand alone
I am part of a greater whole
I am a perfect link
In an endless chain of beings

I quieten the din
I hear the voice within
I stand still
I hear the whisper in the wind

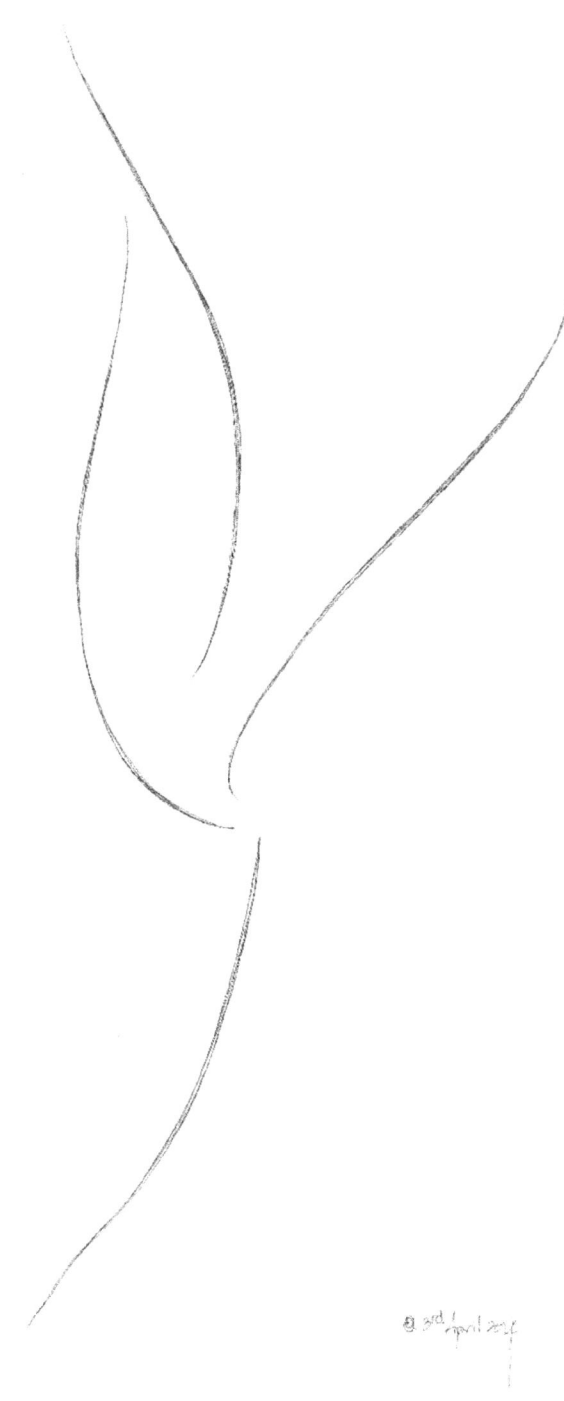

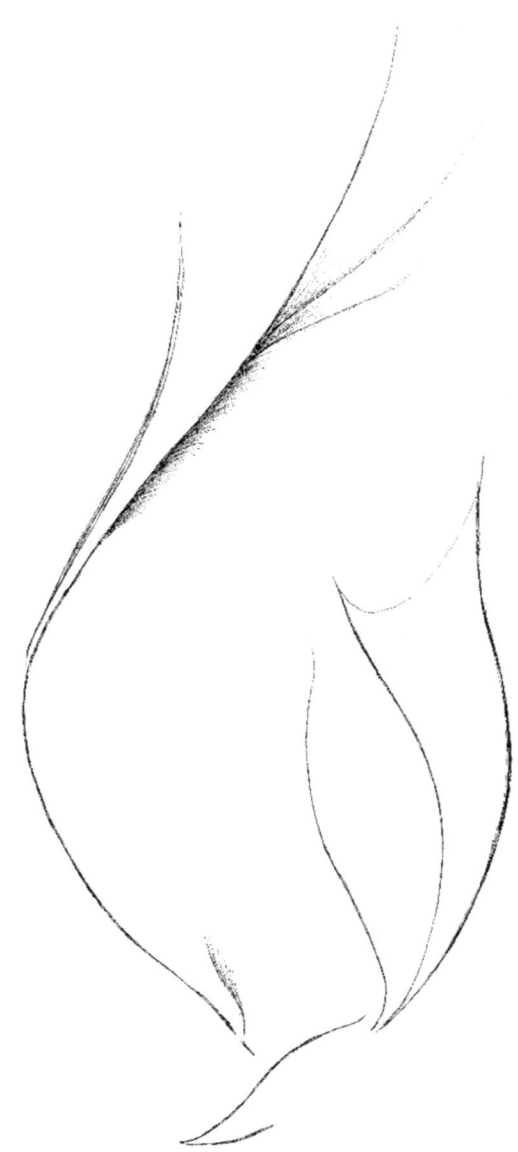

Through storm and gale
A willow stands
A willow

Through my obstacles and challenges
I stand
Me

I run
I hide
From sorrow and pain
They still find me
I weep
I wail

                Today when sorrow knocks
                I open the door
                We sit for a time
                Until it's time to say goodbye

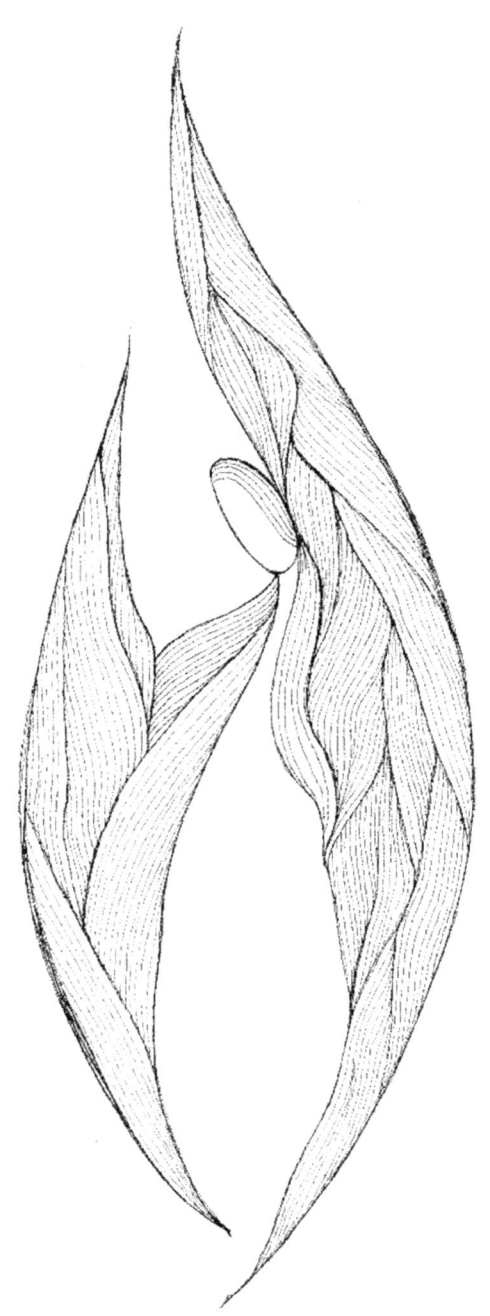

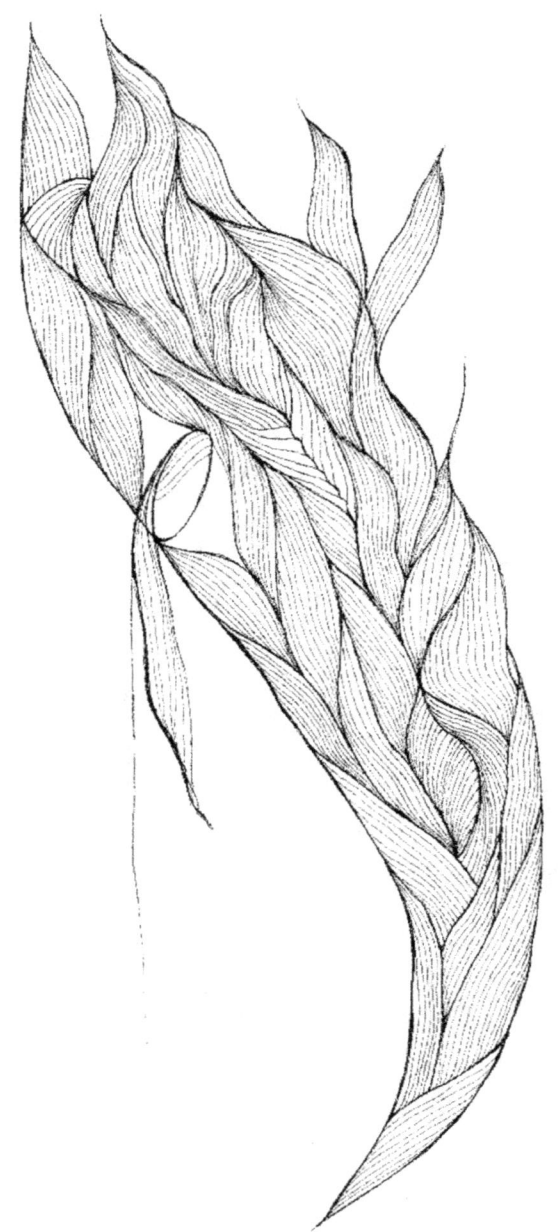

Without fear
Would I recognize love
With fear as my guide
I find love

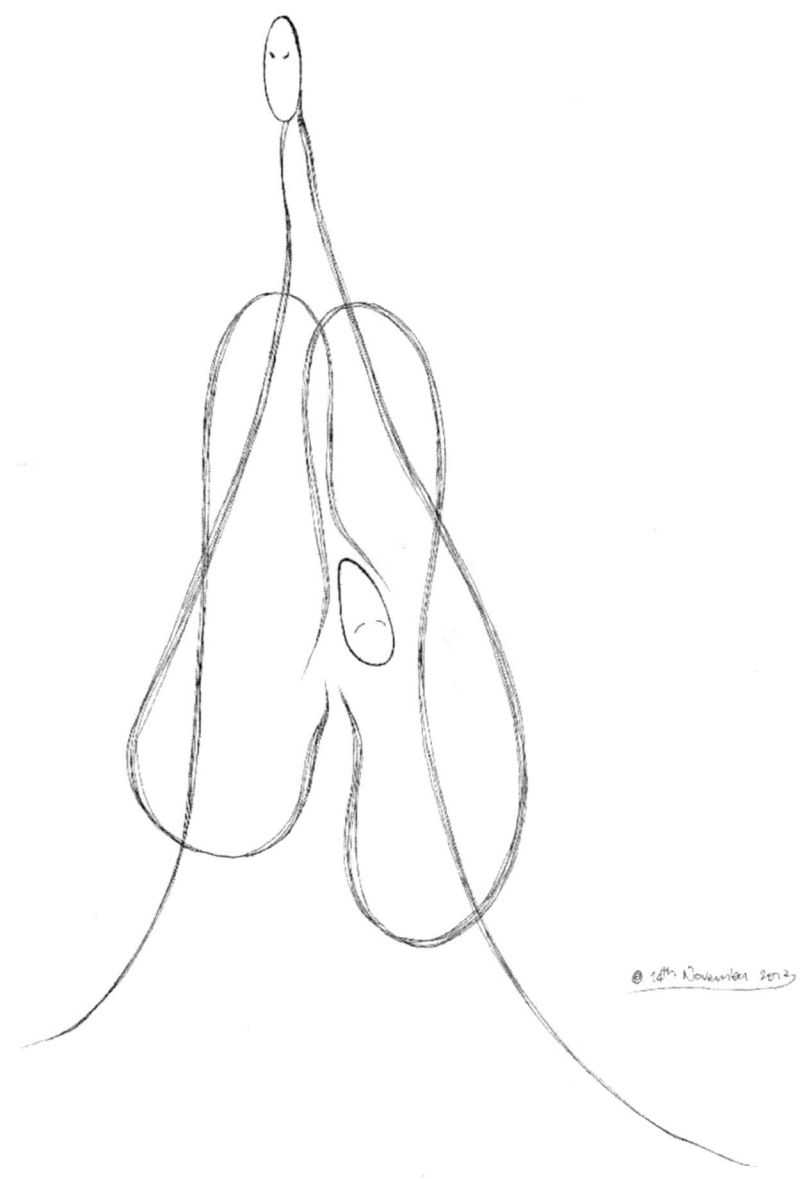

I hang the best pictures on my wall
My worst I trash them all
The memories ….
                    …. Refuse to stray
Now I hang my worst next to my best
For all of them are parts of me

I should have…
If I could turn back the clock…
What if…

It is already done
It is already past
It is already mere shadow

I walk a different path
Does that make me wrong?
I take a different view
Does that make me right?

It just makes me ... me

Don't mourn with me
It does not make my sadness any lesser
Don't worry with me
It does not make my burden any lighter

© 15th November 2013

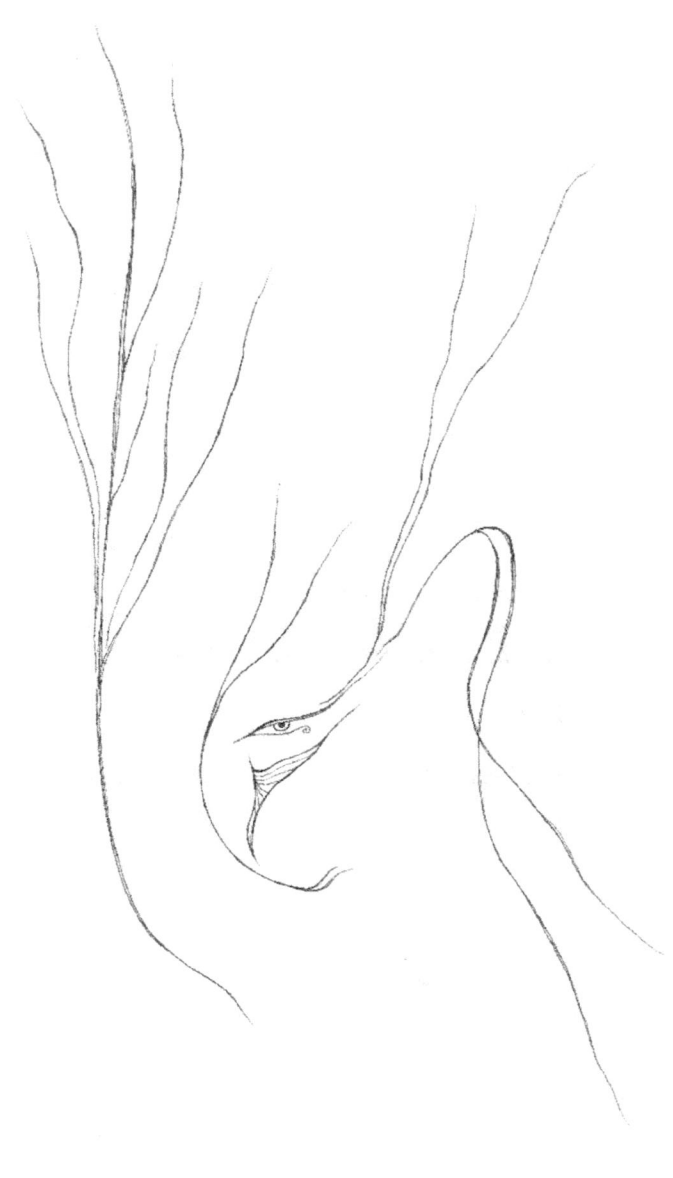

*I can choose to be a victim of my own obstacles
And whine and complain
I can choose to be a judge of my own challenges
And allocate the blame*

I was not born to be a norm
I was not born to be statistic
I was not born ordinary
I was born .... me

I learnt to love
I learnt to fear
I have found my way home
Now I am free

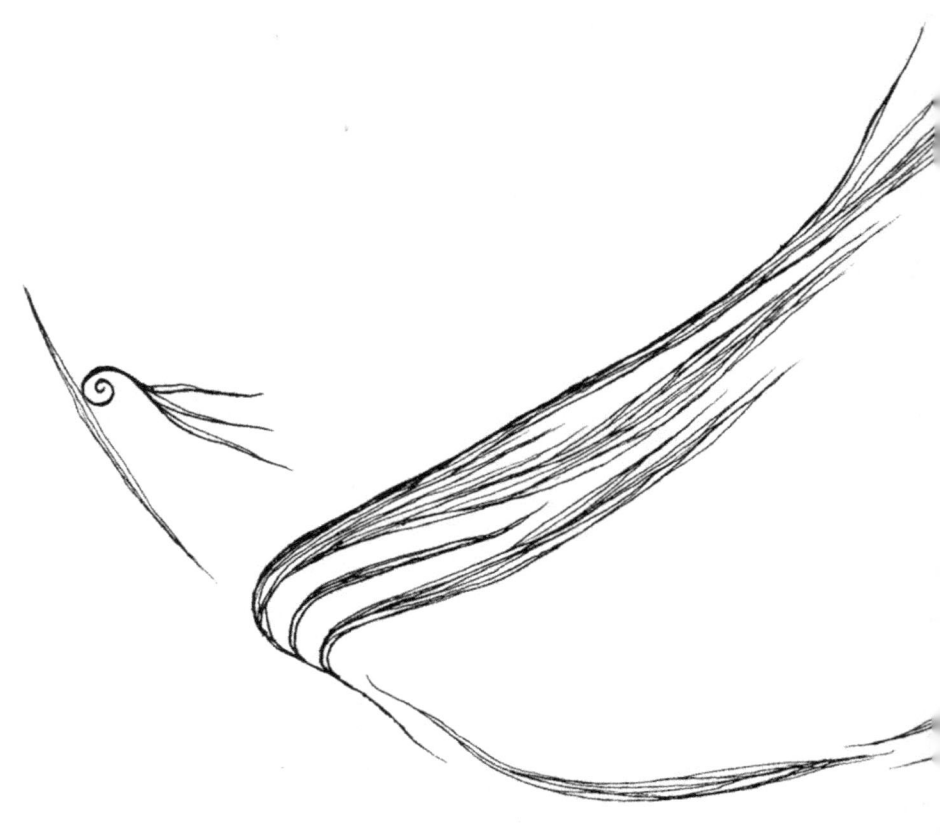

I was proud
I was arrogant
Now I recognize
Humility
In the face of arrogance

There are imperfections
In all perfections

Slowly I break free
Out of the protection of my cocoon
My wings are all the colours of the rainbow
I am beautiful

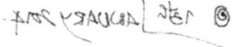

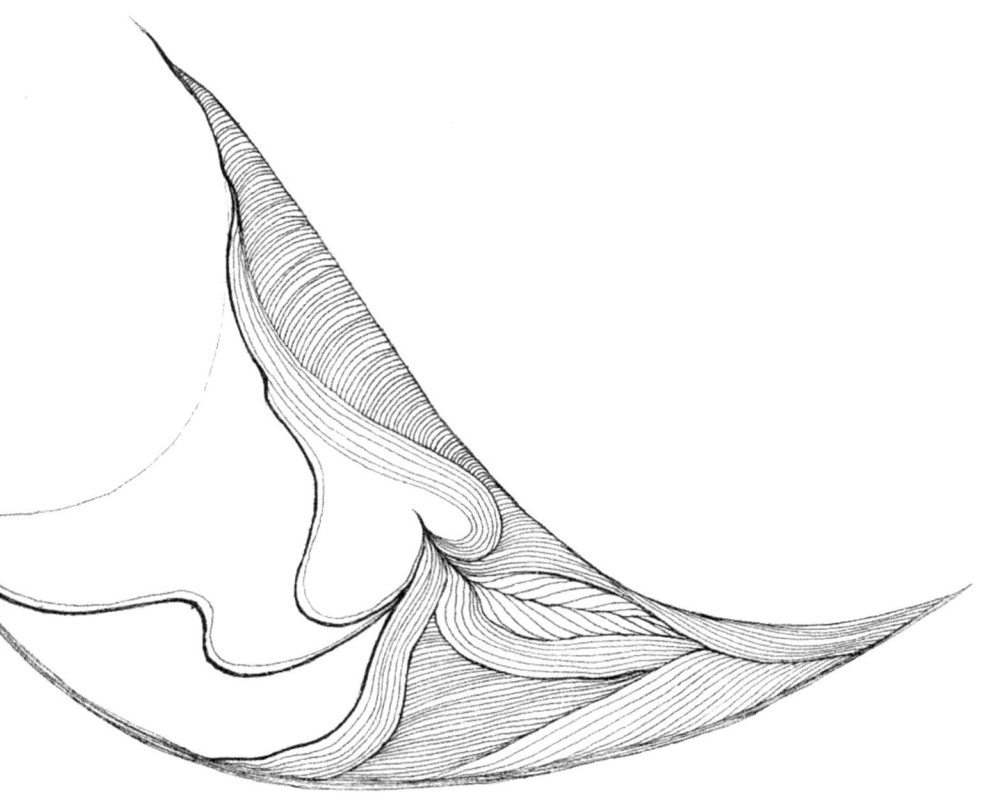

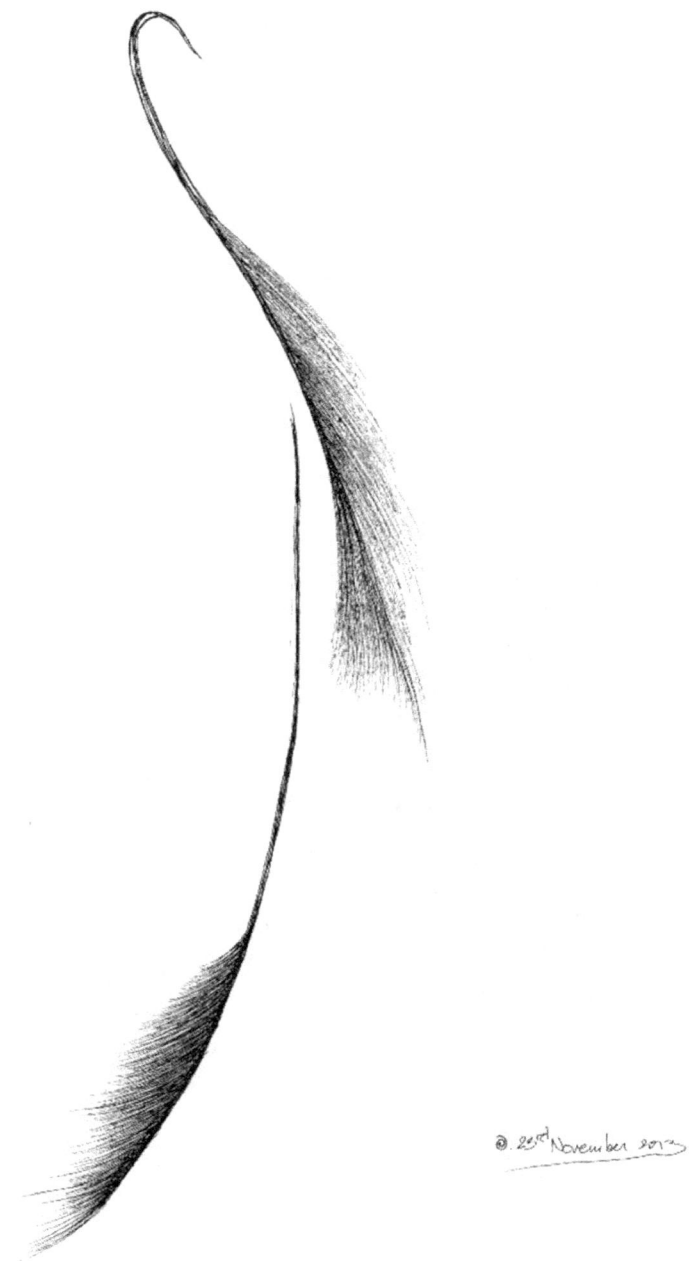

The willow sways in the breeze
Kissing the kesidang
Laughing with ease
The wind dies down
The willow is still
Just being …. Within

What if
What if it is neither bad nor good
What if it is neither black nor white
What if it is neither right nor wrong
What if it is just the wind passing through
What if it doesn't matter at all

I am free

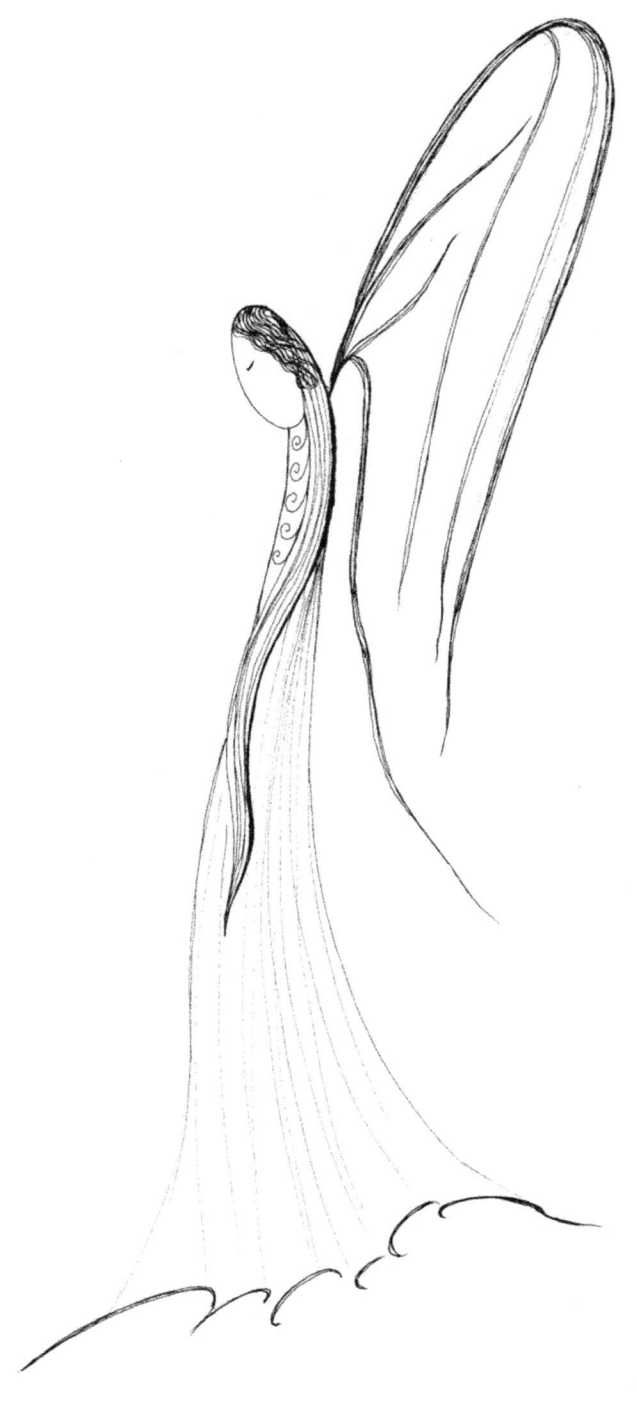

I was lost
I was scared
Now I've found my path
And it is clearer by the day

Life is hard
Life is easy
Life is beautiful
Life is unfair

Life is whatever I choose it to be

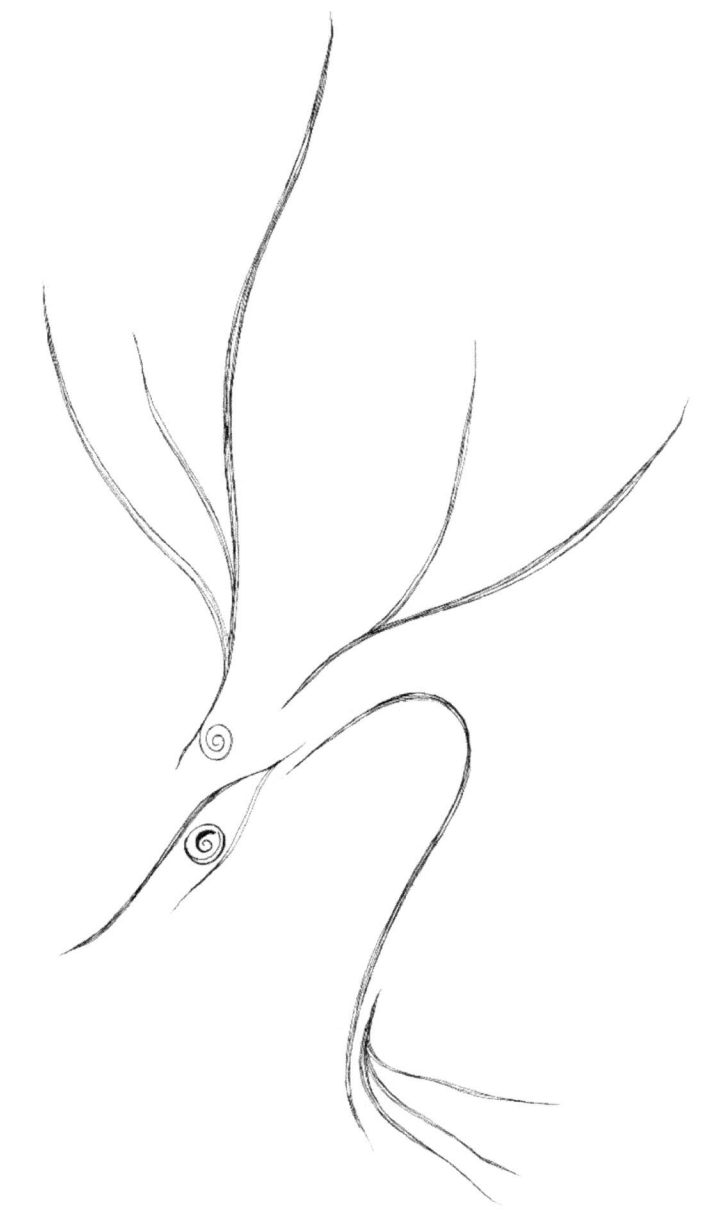

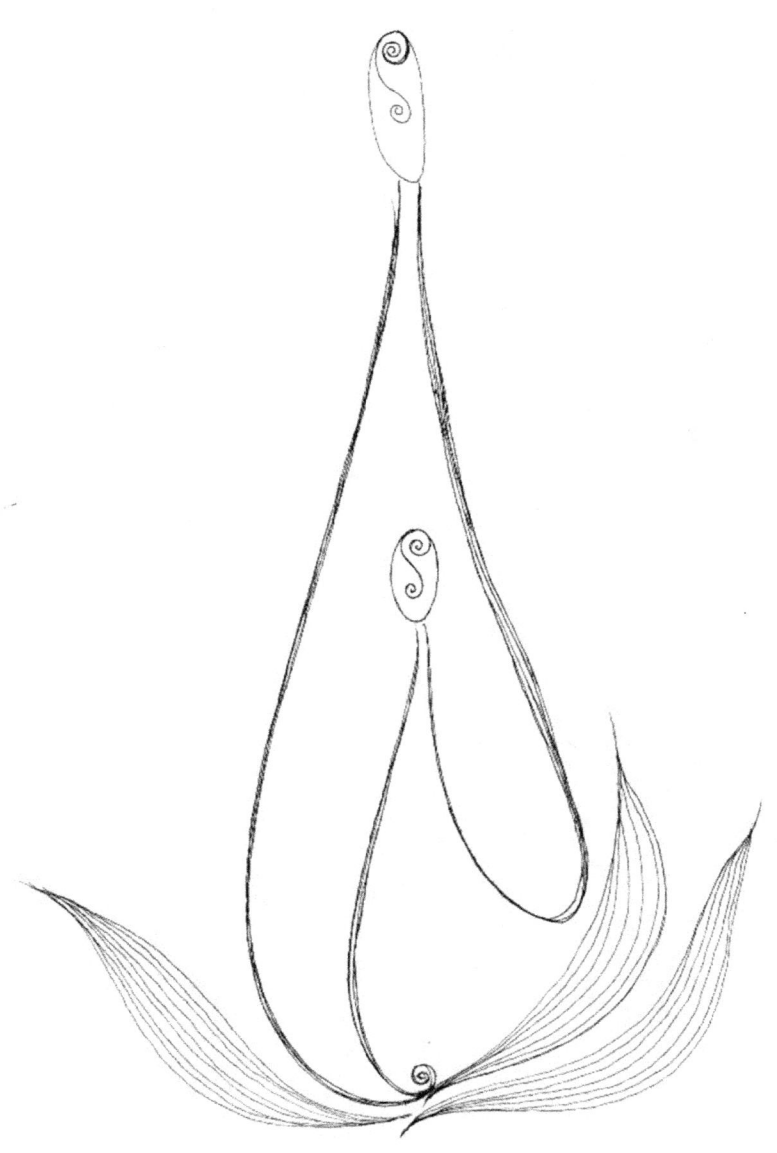

*There is a light shining within me
I see the same light
Shining inside you too*

In death
In life
I am home

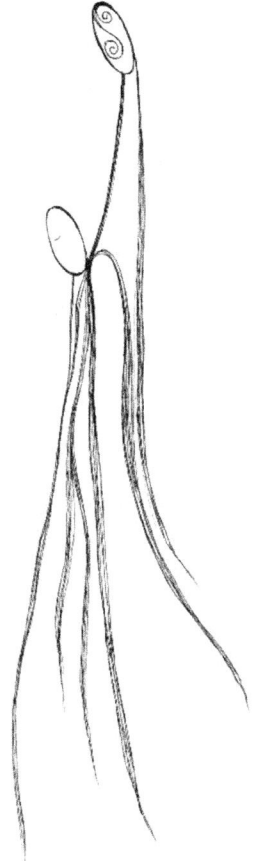

No longer do I dance to the beat of my past

I cannot be angry with you
I cannot take away your pain
I cannot cry for you
Instead …
I am here
And just love you

I sit
I watch
The clouds roll by
Won't you join me
And sit down by my side

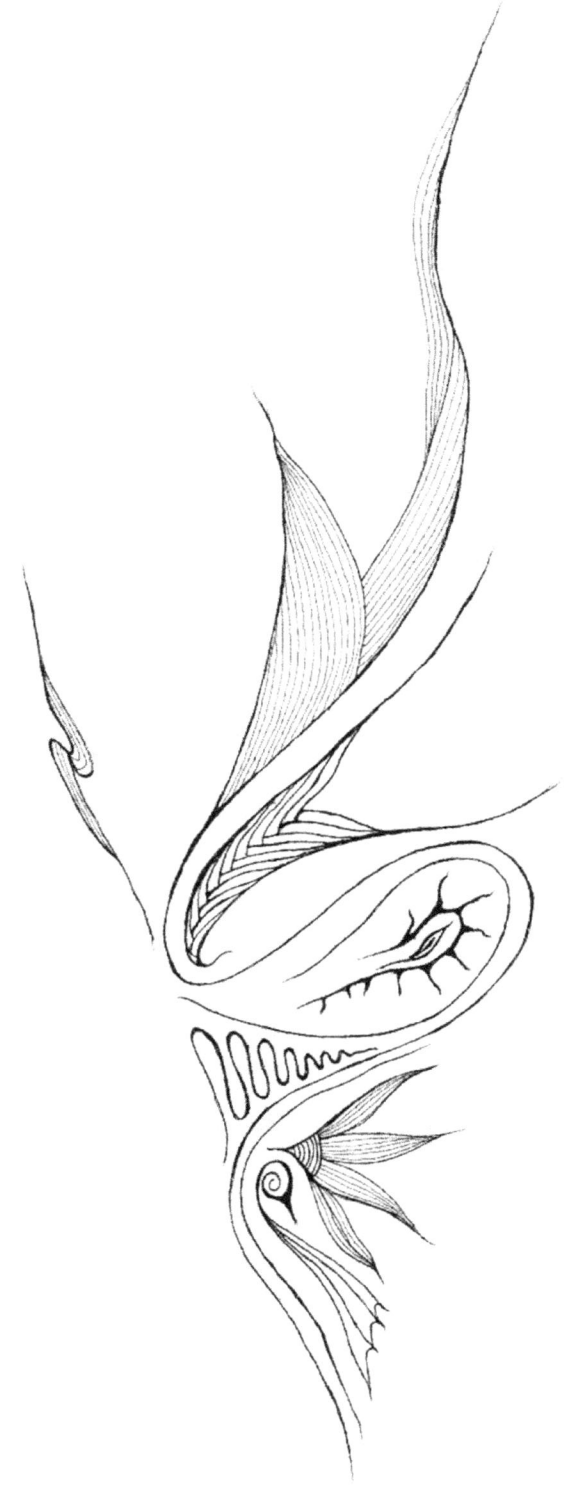

I lived the image I created
Hoping for approval
Hoping for acceptance

I forgive myself for living that way

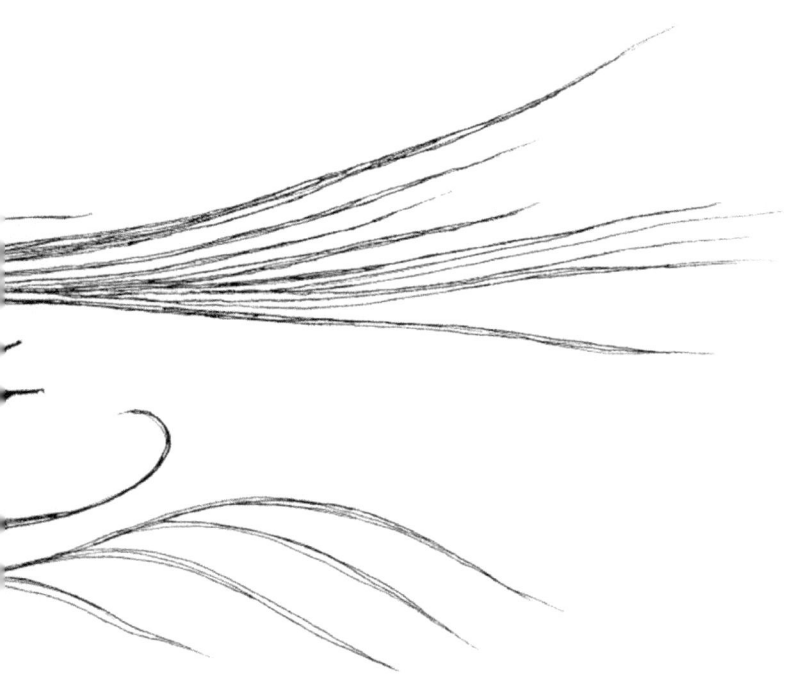

All that crying
The sadness never leaves

All that shouting
The anger still remains

All that repaying
The guilt just gets deeper

I let it all go

It is too hot
It is too dry
It is too wet
I stop …
I breathe …
…. And it is a perfect day

Angel, I call upon thee
Yes, I reply

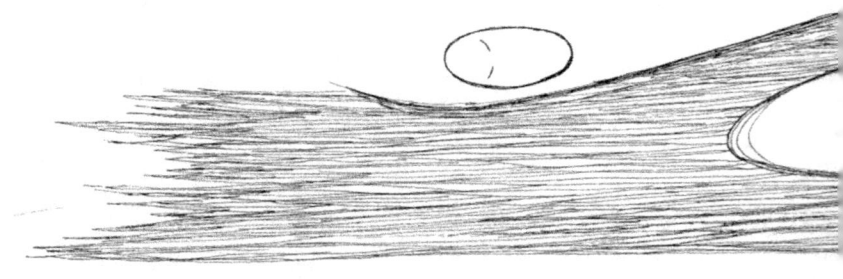

used to be …
i wanted to be a lot of things
used to be …
i wanted to do a lot more
used to be …
i wanted approval and appreciation

used to be …
being me was not enough

From my heart
I emerge
True and strong

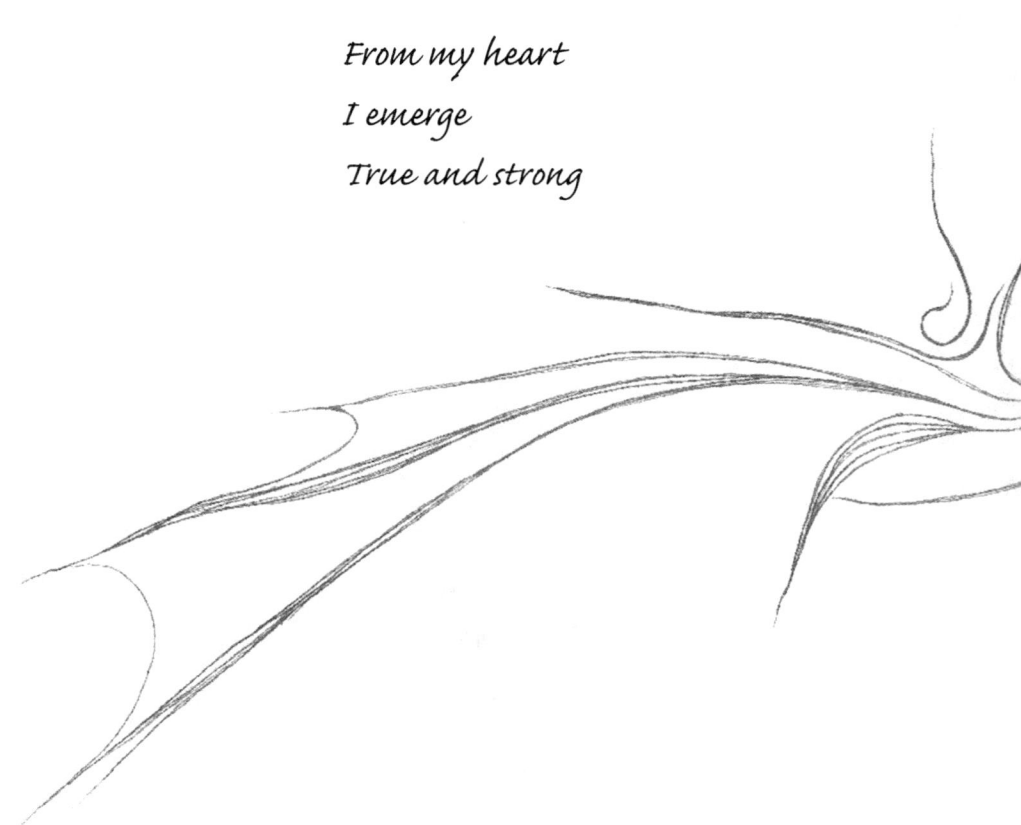

When I see myself without judgment
That's when I truly see you

The whale song
The soul song
The world song
One song

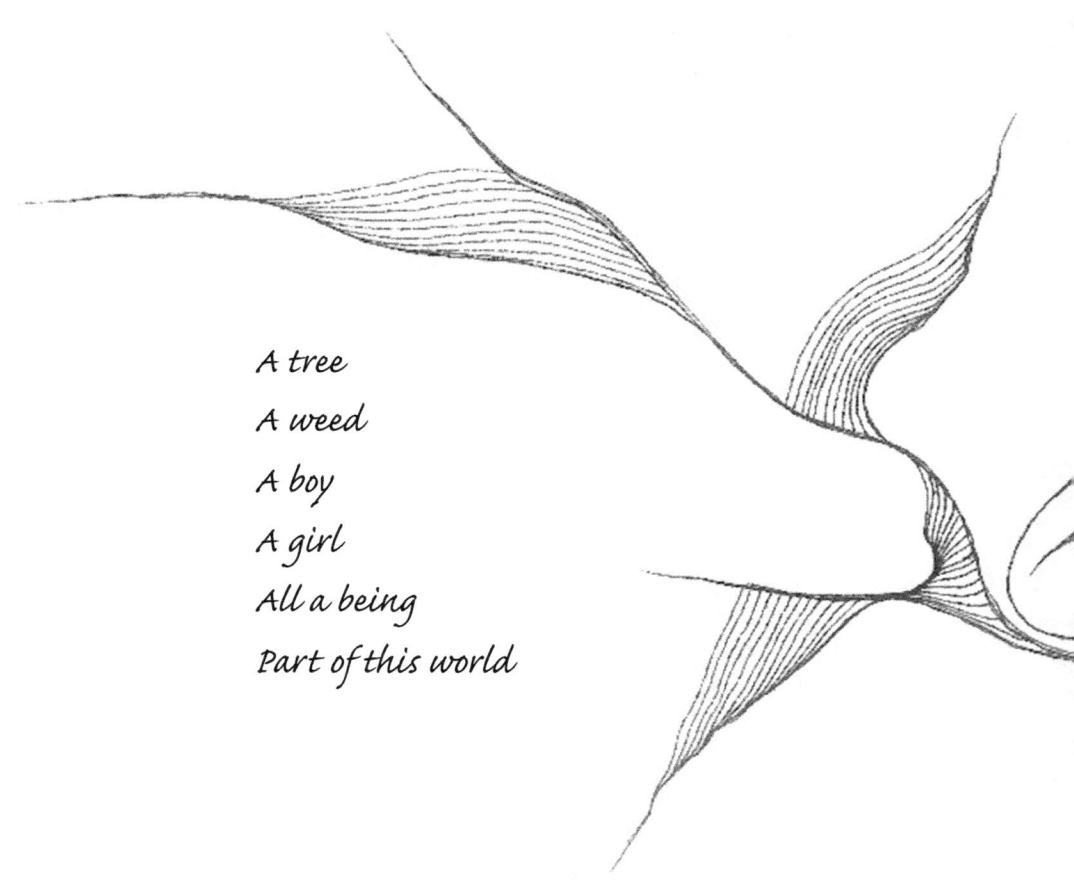

A tree
A weed
A boy
A girl
All a being
Part of this world

© 29th February 2014

My child...

You are free to be whatever you want to be
You are free to do whatever you want to do

I gave birth to you
But your life is not mine to shape

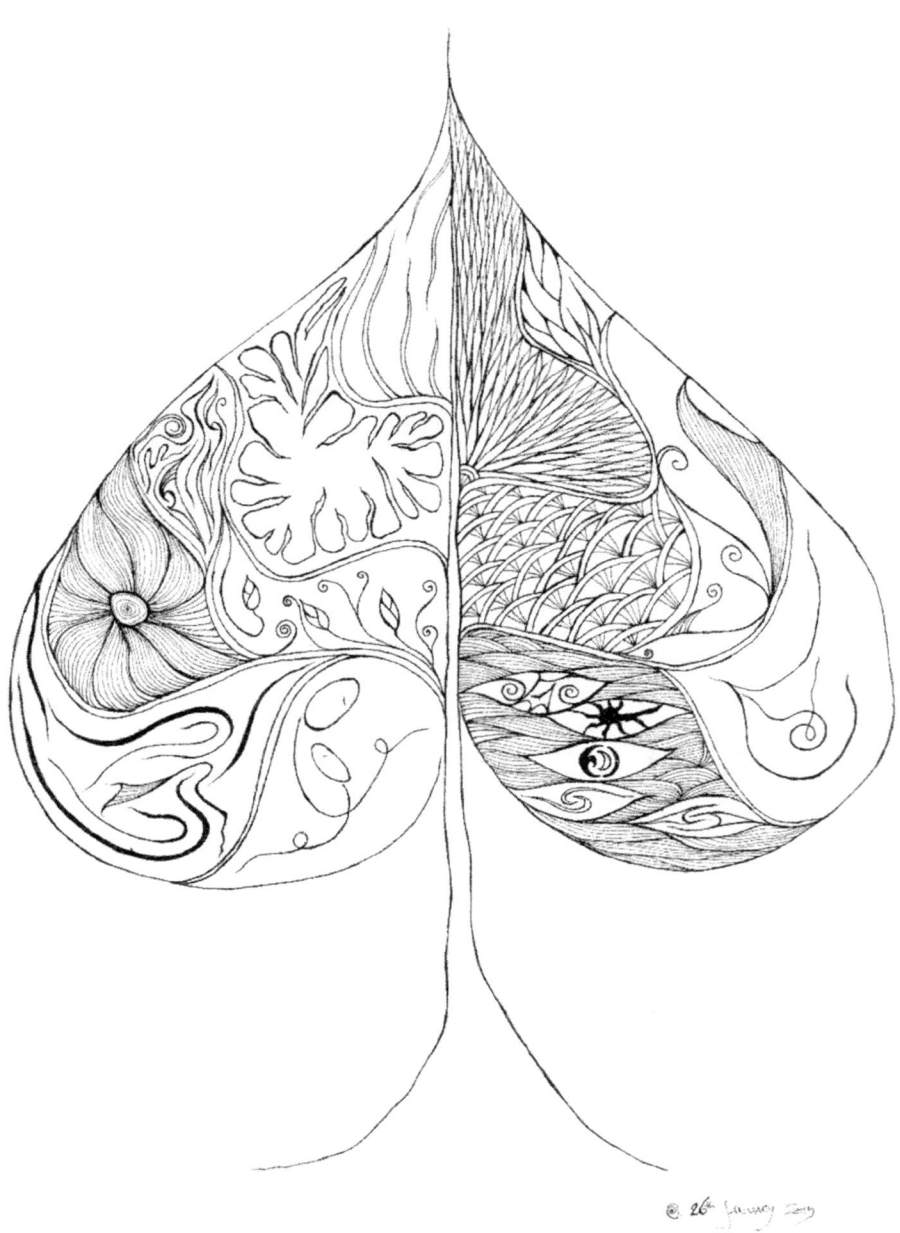

You fall down
I put out my hand

Know this, my daughter
whether you take my hand
is your choice to make
my choice is to put out my hand

A conscious choice is not an IOU and
a you-owe-me

Come sit in my garden
And feel the breeze
Come sit in my garden
And feel our hearts beat

I transform myself
I transform my world

Body
Mind
soul

Synchronicity

I walk up the stream
To find the source
I follow the smoke
To find the fire

It matters not who you are
It is what I hold you to be

I thought I was protecting you
But I was the one afraid of hurt
I thought I wanted the best for you
But I was the one expecting you to be grateful

How I hated myself when I saw what I was like ... within

Fear leads me not forward
Backward it takes me
…. into my soul

Caught in the wind
It takes me high
It takes me low
I grasp and I flail
I fight to break free

I stop
I feel it on my skin
As it passes me by on its way

I laid blames on others
For all the wrongs in my life
I gave credits to others
For all the rights
I sat on the fence
Of my so-called life

.... No longer

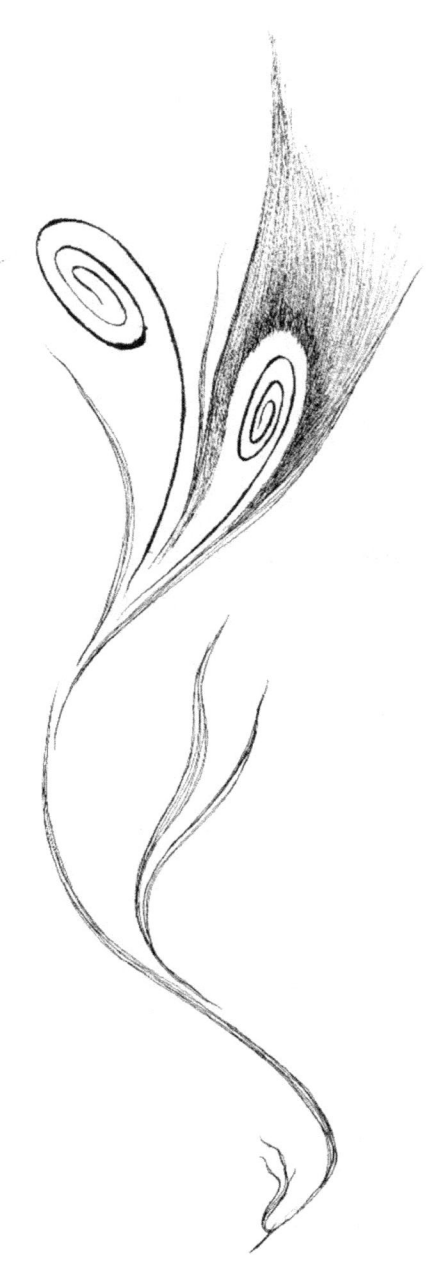

I go by the name of Anna
But I know what I truly am

www.ingramcontent.com/pod-product-compliance
Lightning Source LLC
Chambersburg PA
CBHW052114110526
44592CB00013B/1613